FROM HAND TO MOUTH

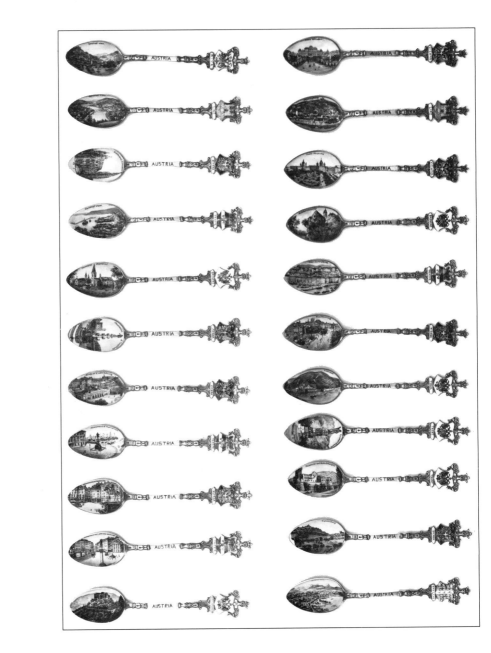

JAMES CROSS GIBLIN

FROM HAND TO MOUTH

Or, How We Invented Knives, Forks, Spoons, and Chopsticks
& the Table Manners To Go With Them

Illustrated with Photographs, Prints, and Drawings

Thomas Y. Crowell   New York

Frontispiece:
Silver souvenir spoons from Austria, 19th century.
Courtesy of The Metropolitan Museum of Art,
Gift of Sir W. H. Redding, 1908

From Hand to Mouth: Or, How We Invented Knives, Forks,
Spoons, and Chopsticks & the Table Manners To Go With Them

Copyright © 1987 by James Cross Giblin
Printed in U.S.A. All rights reserved.
Designed by Bettina Rossner
2   3   4   5   6   7   8   9   10

Library of Congress Cataloging-in-Publication Data
Giblin, James.
    From hand to mouth, or, How we invented knives, forks,
spoons, and chopsticks & the table manners to go with them.

    Bibliography: p.
    Includes index.
    Summary: A history of the eating utensils and table
manners of various cultures from the Stone Age to the
present day.
    1. Flatware—History—Juvenile literature.
2. Table etiquette—History—Juvenile literature.
3. Dinners and dining—History—Juvenile literature.
[1. Flatware—History. 2. Tableware—History. 3. Eating
customs—History.   4. Table etiquette—History.
5. Dinners and dining—History]   I. Title.   II. Title:
How we invented knives, forks, spoons, and chopsticks and
the table manners to go with them.
GT2948.G53 1987   394.1′2′09   86-29341
ISBN 0-690-04660-X
ISBN 0-690-04662-6 (lib. bdg.)

Acknowledgments

For their help in providing research material and illustrations,
the author thanks the following individuals and institutions:

Bayerisches Nationalmuseum, Munich
Alice Belgray
The Bettman Archive
The Cleveland Museum of Art
Cooper-Hewitt Museum of Design, Smithsonian Institution
Mary Elting
Elizabeth Isele
The Library of Congress
The Metropolitan Museum of Art
Jim Murphy
The New York Public Library
The New York Times
Lila Perl
Jeanne Prahl
Bebe Faas Rice
UPI Newsphotos

and special thanks to my editor, Barbara Fenton

ALSO BY JAMES CROSS GIBLIN

Milk
The Fight for Purity

The Truth About Santa Claus

Chimney Sweeps
Yesterday and Today

The Skyscraper Book

For Murray

Contents

CHAPTER ONE

Flint Knives and Fingers

IT IS A COOL SPRING EVENING 15,000 years ago, and a fire blazes
outside the entrance to a cave in what is today southern France.
Huddled around the fire is a small group of Stone Age men,
women, and children. They are roasting chunks of bison meat
impaled on the ends of sharpened sticks. The meat sizzles as
they poke the sticks back and forth, being careful not to let
them catch fire.

When a piece seems to be done, the man who cooked it
pulls it quickly away from the flames. The meat is too hot for
the man to grab with his fingers, but he is hungry and doesn't
want to wait until it cools. So he reaches for the sharp flint
knife that he keeps under the belt of his skin clothing. Poking
the knife into the tough, sinewy meat, he removes it from the
stick and brings it to his mouth.

Flint knives like the one the man used have been found with the remains of Stone Age people all across western Europe. Some are more than 100,000 years old. With them, people skinned animals they killed in the hunt and cut the meat into manageable pieces. Sometimes they may have used their knives in eating, as the man did, but most people of the time ate only with their fingers. And many people in the world still do.

Eskimos of the far north who follow the old ways gather around the stewpot, cooking over a seal-oil fire in the center of the family's igloo. The men of the family eat first, dipping

A schoolgirl in northern India eats lunch with her fingers.

Courtesy of UPI/ Bettmann Newsphotos

their fingers into the pot and pulling out the biggest pieces of caribou meat. The women and children follow, searching the pot for the smaller pieces the men have left behind.

In southern India, people often pile their meals of rice, chicken, and vegetables on banana leaves and use all of their fingers while eating. Indians of the north use only the fingers of their right hand, and are careful never to get food on their fingers above the first knuckle. To do so is considered bad manners.

Both southern and northern Indians wash their hands thoroughly before eating, often in special finger bowls.

Arab nomads of the desert also eat with their fingers. An Arab family will sit down to a single large tray or platter of rice surrounded by bowls of mutton, chicken, or camel meat. The rice is sticky enough to be grasped in clumps.

Arabs eat only with the fingers of their right hands, although they may hold a piece of chicken or lamb with the left. This is an age-old sanitary measure, since people in the Arab world have traditionally used the fingers of their left hands to wipe themselves after defecating.

In Ethiopia, where food is often in short supply, people bake a round, flat kind of bread called *injera.* It is made from millet flour and can be as much as two feet in diameter. Ethiopians put the injera on a tray and cover it with a reddish sauce flavored with onions and spices. If chicken, lamb, or beef are available, chunks of them are dropped into the sauce.

Arabs eating a meal of rice and vegetables.

Courtesy of the Picture Collection, Cooper-Hewitt Museum, Smithsonian Institution/ Art Resource

Before beginning to eat, Ethiopians always wash their hands. During the meal they break off pieces of injera from around the edge and use them to scoop up the sauce and the morsels of meat. They keep eating in this way until the last bit of injera is gone. Then they wash their hands again. Like the Arabs and the people of northern India, Ethiopians use only the fingers of the right hand in eating.

While millions of people throughout the world continue to eat with their fingers, millions of others rely on utensils. The development of these utensils took thousands and thousands of years. Starting with knives, people in the Near and Far East went on to invent spoons, chopsticks, and finally forks.

With the introduction of forks, people became more self-conscious about their eating habits. They decided there were right and wrong ways to eat, and listed them in guides to table manners. Over the years, these guides became more and more elaborate.

This book tells the intriguing story behind our everyday eating utensils and the table manners that grew up alongside them. It begins far back in the prehistoric past when some unknown man or woman first saw the possibilities of the spoon.

CHAPTER TWO

Ancient Spoons and Knives

A FAMILY HAS GATHERED for their evening meal in the courtyard of their mud-brick house. The house is one of several hundred in a village on the shores of the eastern Mediterranean Sea in what is today Israel. Although it is almost 5000 years ago, people are already living in settled communities, raising crops each year, making pottery, and tending flocks of cattle, sheep, and goats.

The mother of the family puts a steaming pot of soup on a low wooden table and ladles it into individual clay bowls. She serves the father first, then the grandfather and grandmother, and finally the four children and herself. The soup smells delicious. It is thickened with barley and contains onions, carrots, and chunks of baby lamb. The family members lift their bowls and eagerly dip into the soup with spoons made from seashells.

Historians agree that the spoon is our oldest eating utensil. Only the knife is an older implement, and as we have seen, it was not developed originally for eating.

Ancient peoples probably got the idea for spoons from the shells of clams and mussels that they picked up along the banks of rivers and the shores of lakes and oceans. Some of the shells could be used as found, but most of them had to be polished and shaped.

Every spoon consists of two parts: the bowl, which contains the solid or liquid food, and the stem, or handle, which the diner grips. The shells of a sea creature, the cowrie, formed the bowls of some spoons dating from 1500 B.C. that have been unearthed in Egypt. The shells were mounted on stems of wood or bone. The family portrayed in the opening scene of this chapter ate with similar spoons, and they were common throughout the ancient Middle East.

Other early spoons were carved from wood. One of the oldest, found at a burial site near Lucerne, Switzerland, was made between 3000 and 2500 B.C. It's interesting to note that our word "spoon" comes from the old Anglo-Saxon word *spon*, which meant a chip or splinter of wood. This seems to indicate that most of the spoons used by the ancient peoples of northern Europe were wooden.

Another favorite material of early spoon makers was horn. The curved horns of sheep or goats made excellent oval-shaped spoons when they were properly cut and fastened to a stem of wood, bone, or another piece of horn. Larger animal horns could be softened by boiling and then pressed into the shape of spoons, with the stem and bowl in one piece. Examples of both types of horn spoons, dating back to 2000 B.C. and earlier, have been found in Turkey and other countries.

While people were eating with spoons made of shell, wood, or horn, they were still cutting their food with flint knives.

Flint knives from prehistoric Egypt.

Courtesy of The Metropolitan Museum of Art, Rogers Fund, 1907 and 1910

These were similar to the knives their Stone Age ancestors had used thousands of years before.

Flint is a kind of stone that is harder than many metals. It was formed more than 100 million years ago when sponges with glassy skeletons thrived at the bottom of the seas that covered much of what is now western Europe. As the earth rose and the seas retreated, enormous pressure solidified the sponge skeletons into layers of flint.

Prehistoric people found pieces of flint on the earth's surface and saw that the fresh edges were very sharp. They learned how to chip, grind, and polish the flint into even sharper and more efficient spear points and knives. Later they discovered that the best flint for making knives and other tools came from deep underground. They dug mines to obtain it, and a brisk trade in high-quality flint developed in the ancient world.

From western Europe to the Middle East, people hunted, cooked, and ate with knives made of flint. The Egyptians sometimes carved wooden knives with a slot into which they glued a cutting edge of flint. Other Egyptian flint knives had elaborately decorated handles of bone or ivory.

Many examples of flint knives can still be seen in museums, but few ancient spoons made of shell, wood, or horn have survived. Most of those spoons have long since rotted or crumbled into dust. It wasn't until people learned to work with copper and other metals that they were able to fashion spoons and other utensils that would last—not just for a lifetime, but for centuries.

Perhaps people first discovered metallic ores when hot fires melted some out of the hearthstones that were in almost constant use for heating and cooking. However it happened, we know that as far back as 9000 B.C. people in what is now Turkey were extracting copper from its ore by heating, or smelting. They shaped the copper into bowls, ornaments, and weapons.

Sometime later, people in the Middle East and Asia learned how to make a much harder metal, bronze, by heating copper and tin until they melted and mixed together. When the molten metal cooled and hardened, bronze was formed.

Egyptian bronze knives with wooden handles from the 18th Dynasty (1570–1342 B.C.).

Courtesy of The Metropolitan Museum of Art, Rogers Fund, 1925

Ancient metalworkers produced knives of bronze by pouring the hot, liquid metal into clay or stone molds and letting it set. This process is known as casting, and knife and sword

molds found in the Middle East reveal that it was being practiced as early as 3500 B.C.

While bronze was a more versatile metal than copper, it had its limitations. For one thing, the materials necessary for its manufacture—especially tin—were quite scarce in the ancient world.

Iron ore was much more common, but for a long time people didn't know how to make it into good, strong iron. Then about 1400 B.C. the Hittites, a people who lived in what is now Syria, invented the process known as forging. In this process, iron ore was heated again and again and hammered into the desired shape. Then it was plunged into cold water. This hardened the metal, enabling knife makers to give it a keen, durable cutting edge.

The Hittites tried to keep their ironworking techniques a secret so that they could retain a monopoly on the manufacture of high-quality swords, daggers, and knives. But after the downfall of the Hittite empire in 1200 B.C., knowledge of iron

Ancient Egyptian spoons made of bronze.

Courtesy of The Metropolitan Museum of Art, Gift of Egypt Exploration Fund, 1897

technology spread quickly throughout the Middle East and southern Europe.

As metalworkers experimented with iron, they discovered that it could be strengthened even more if it was mixed, or alloyed, with carbon and other elements. The workers put the iron and carbon into a container called a crucible and heated them at very high temperatures until they melted and fused together. The result was steel.

Swords and knives made of steel were extremely strong and extremely sharp. In fact the Spartans, who lived in ancient Greece, are said to have owed their success in war to the steel swords they began carrying into battle around 650 B.C.

Although bronze, iron, and steel were probably employed first in the manufacture of weapons, they were soon put to more peaceful uses. Jewelry, mirrors, pots, and kitchen knives were all made from the new metals. And so were spoons. Starting about 1000 B.C., the Egyptians produced small, round bronze spoons with a sharp point at the end of the stems. Perhaps a diner turned the spoon around and used the point to spear pieces of meat or fish. Or perhaps he extracted snails from their shells with it. No one today knows for sure.

Ancient spoons were usually shaped by casting. This could be done in either a permanent mold of stone or a temporary one made of clay. When a stone mold was used, molten bronze or iron was poured into it and allowed to set. Then the two parts of the mold were separated, and the spoon was removed.

Making a spoon in a temporary mold was more complicated. First the design of the spoon was molded carefully in wax. Then the wax model was embedded in damp clay with a small hole left at one end. After the clay block dried and hardened, it was heated to a high temperature. The wax ran out, and molten metal replaced it in the clay mold. When the metal had cooled and set, the mold was chipped away.

This process, called the "lost wax method," is still used in the manufacture of some spoons today. It is slow and expensive, because a new wax pattern has to be created for each spoon. But the bowl of the spoon can be cast very thin in the lost wax method, and the stem can be given extra-fine detailing.

The Romans, whose empire was at its peak at the time of Christ, used both methods of casting to make their bronze and silver spoons.

Two basic types of Roman spoons have been found in the ruins of Pompeii and other ancient towns and cities. One, with a round bowl and a long, thin stem ending in a point, bears a strong resemblance to early Egyptian spoons. Its purpose is made clear in a Roman wall painting that shows such a spoon resting across a bowl of eggs.

According to a Roman superstition, evil spirits often lurked inside fresh eggs. Many Romans believed that before they cracked open and ate an egg, they should pierce the shell so the evil spirits could escape. The sharp point at the end of the first type of spoon was perfectly designed to do this.

The other type of Roman spoon, called the *ligula*, looked much like our modern spoons. It had an oval bowl and a narrow, rounded stem that often ended in a decoration. The stems of some ligulas were also inscribed with sayings, such as "Use me with happiness," "Live well," and "Live to conquer." The last one probably appeared on a spoon made for an army officer.

The Romans observed an elaborate set of table manners throughout their vast empire, which stretched from Britain in the west to Central Asia in the east. They loved grand banquets with many courses. Between courses, they washed their hands in silver finger bowls and wiped them on linen napkins.

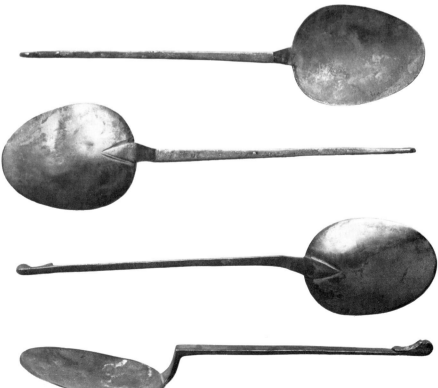

Roman spoons of gold and silver in the ligula *style. Note decoration in the form of a duck head and bill at the ends of the stems.*

Courtesy of The Metropolitan Museum of Art, Rogers Fund, 1920

A Roman banquet scene as imagined by a 19th-century illustrator.

All that came to an end with the collapse of the Roman Empire in western Europe in A.D. 476. In some parts of Europe the use of eating utensils and the state of table manners fell back to an almost prehistoric level. And they remained on that level for hundreds of years.

⊠⊠⊠⊠

CHAPTER THREE

Don't Put Your Whole Hand in the Pot!

MISTS ARE GATHERING around the high stone walls of the duke's castle in northern France on a chilly November evening. Inside, servants light torches in the castle's great hall, signaling that the evening meal is about to begin.

A long board has been laid on trestles in the middle of the room and covered with tablecloths. On one side of the board, the cloth goes all the way to the stone floor to prevent the duke's dogs from crawling under the table in search of scraps. On the other side is a single long bench for all the diners to sit on. The year is A.D. 1200, and neither permanent dining tables nor individual chairs are common yet, even in the homes of the wealthy.

Against the wall is a smaller serving table crowded with jugs of wine, joints of meat, and steaming bowls of soup and stew. At one end of this table sits a bronze container of water, along with a matching basin and a towel.

The container is called an *aquamanile*, which means it is used for the washing of hands. Aquamaniles were often made in playful forms like this one, which shows a dragon swallowing a man. The curve of the dragon's tail makes a handle and the water flows out from a hole beneath the man's head.

As the diners enter the hall, they first stop by the side table

Aquamanile of a dragon swallowing a man. German, 12th–13th century.

Courtesy of The Metropolitan Museum of Art, The Cloisters Collection, 1947

to wash their hands at the aquamanile. The washing is done in public so that everyone will know his neighbors' fingers are clean when they reach into a bowl for food.

There are no place settings of utensils to greet the diners when they sit down at the table, nor any napkins. There aren't even any plates. The only things on the table at the start of the meal are bowls for soup, one for each two guests, and spoons to eat it with.

Instead of plates, the diners are handed thick, square slices of four-day-old bread. These are called *trenchers.* When the servants pass by with platters of meat and other dishes, the diners help themselves with their bare hands and put the portions they have taken on their trenchers. At the end of the meal, the gravy-soaked trenchers will be collected and given to poor families on the duke's estate.

The diners keep a finger or two extended while eating so that they'll be free of grease and available for the next course. From this probably comes today's "polite" custom of extending the little finger while holding a spoon or small fork.

Sometimes, rather than use his fingers, a diner will open a leather case he has brought with him and take out his knife. It has a sharp point, like most knives of the time, and with it he can spear pieces of meat and fish from the serving plates.

Not a single person along the table eats with a fork. That utensil isn't yet known in western Europe.

Although a dinner scene like the one just described may seem strange and messy to us today, it was considered perfectly normal in the Middle Ages. Utensils that we take for granted, such as knives and spoons, were much rarer and more expensive then.

A servant cuts trenchers of bread in this banquet scene. Woodcut by German artist M. Wohlgemuth, 1491.

Courtesy of The Metropolitan Museum of Art, Rogers Fund, 1919

The making of knives and other cutting tools became a respected profession in the Middle Ages. From about the year 1200, the cutlery industry was centered at London and Sheffield in England, at Paris and Thiers in France, and at Solingen in Germany. These places all had plentiful timber to heat furnaces and provide charcoal for making steel, as well as the water low in chemicals that was needed for hardening and tempering the metal.

In Sheffield, England, two men working together forged the steel for knives. One, the forger, held the red-hot bar of steel on an anvil with a pair of tongs. He kept twisting and turning the bar while his partner, the hammer-man, beat it with a heavy hammer. Often the men had to reheat the bar several times before they succeeded in reducing it to the right thickness.

After that, the future knife blade was tempered, ground, whetted to a fine, sharp edge, and finally polished. All told, the forged knife blade went through at least twelve separate operations before it was ready for a handle to be attached to the projection, or tang, at its top.

Master cutlers produced elaborate knives for their wealthy customers among the nobility and the clergy. Sometimes the blades were made of silver instead of steel. They had handles of marble, ivory, agate, amber, or gold. Often a design was carved into the handle, or it was inlaid with precious stones.

Steel knife with ivory handle carved in the form of three boy acrobats. Italian, 17th century.

Courtesy of The Metropolitan Museum of Art, Bequest of Alan Rutherfurd Stuyvesant, 1954

Some English table knives of the 1400s were said to have handles made from unicorn horns. Such handles were prized because the horn of a unicorn was believed to act as a charm against poison. The handles probably came from the narwhal, a sea creature with a single long tusk. Until the 1600s, people thought narwhal tusks were really unicorn horns.

Innkeepers didn't provide table knives for their guests in the Middle Ages, and most hosts didn't either. So people took their knives with them when they traveled. The wealthy nobles and clergy carried theirs in handsome sheaths of tooled and decorated leather. Poorer people simply stuck their knives into their belts or a stocking.

In the homes of well-to-do Christians, knives with different-colored handles were used to help celebrate certain religious holidays. For example, knives with black handles made of ebony were brought out during Lent as a symbol of Christ's suffering. Then on Easter, knives with white handles made of ivory symbolized His resurrection.

Because knives in the Middle Ages had sharp points and could be used as weapons as well as utensils, firm rules developed about the way they were handled during meals. A French book of instruction for college students advised the person in charge of the dining hall to say at the start of each meal, "Every man draw his knife!" and at the end of the meal, "Every man clean his knife and replace it in his sheath!" That way no knives would be left lying around the table when not in use.

Other rules said that a knife should always be placed on the table with the sharp edge facing in toward the diner rather than out toward his neighbor. It should never be lifted from the table during courses when it wasn't needed. And if it were offered to someone else, the knife should be held by the point instead of the handle so that it wouldn't seem threatening.

Spoons, like knives, were often objects of great value in the Middle Ages. Starting in the 1200s, they began to be listed in the wills and household inventories of rich people. From these lists, we know that spoons were carved from all kinds of woods, especially boxwood, juniper, poplar, and cherry. They were also cast from brass, bronze, silver, and gold.

Sometimes the tops of the stems were ornamented with precious stones. Other stems bore the owner's coat-of-arms. On some spoons the stem was attached to the bowl with a small, sculpted head of a dog, a lion, or a dragon.

Because cheaper metals could be given a thin coating of silver and passed off as the real thing, King Edward I of England laid down a standard for silver spoons and other articles. In order to be described as made of silver, they had to contain at least 92.5 percent of the valuable metal. The King ordered the wardens of Goldsmiths' Hall in London to examine all silver articles to make sure they met the standard. Those that passed the test were marked with a leopard's head on the back of the stem. Other cities had different marks, but all of them came to be known as "hallmarks" because the first ones were applied at Goldsmiths' Hall in the 1300s.

While spoons made for the rich often seemed more like jewels than utensils, those used by the poor were made of wood or a cheap metal like tin or pewter. Traveling tinsmiths

A Dutch peasant family saying grace before eating their dinner of soup. Etching by A. van Ostade (1610–1685).

Courtesy of The Metropolitan Museum of Art, Rogers Fund, 1917

often molded the crude metal spoons as the children of a peasant family stood by, watching.

Some spoons made by the poor possessed their own special meaning and beauty. Young Norwegian men carved wooden spoons and gave them to girls they liked in hopes that the girls would accept them as suitors. Sometimes the young men made two spoons, joined by a flexible wooden chain.

In Holland, grooms-to-be carved "bride spoons" out of wood and gave them to their fiancées as presents before the wedding. The spoons often carried inscriptions that proclaimed the young man's feelings for his future wife. One of these, scratched in tiny letters on the back of the bowl, read:

My everlasting love,
Accept what I am sending you.
Although it is rather simple,
God knows it comes from the heart.

Metal spoons were now being made by forging as well as casting. In this method, a short metal bar was shaped into a spoon by repeated hammering. An ornament on the stem could be produced by pounding the metal into a die pattern. Sometimes a decorative figure was sculpted separately and soldered onto the end of the stem. That was how the unusual Apostle spoons were made.

Apostle spoons came in sets of thirteen and featured miniature figures of the twelve Apostles sent out by Jesus Christ

Silver Apostle spoon with the figure of St. Jude on the stem. English (London), 1592.

Courtesy of The Metropolitan Museum of Art, Gift of Mr. and Mrs. James B. Mabon, 1967

to teach the gospel. The thirteenth spoon bore the figure of Jesus himself, larger and more beautifully designed than the others.

Apostle spoons first appeared in the 1400s, when the Christians of Europe were deeply religious, and images of Christ, His apostles, and the saints of the Roman Catholic Church could be seen everywhere. It was a time when Christian families said special household prayers before and after every meal, and believed that the apostles had the power to influence their lives.

The spoons were found in all parts of Europe, including France, Germany, Italy, the Low Countries, and Britain. Some were made of silver and were available only in complete sets. Others were made of cheaper metals, such as pewter, and were sold individually. Families handed down their treasured Apostle spoons from generation to generation, and people often gave an Apostle spoon to a newborn baby as a birth present. These spoons were engraved with the child's name and the date and place of birth.

Changes in fashion sometimes dictated the design of spoons. In the late 1500s, both men and women started to wear big, stiff lace collars called ruffs. Before then, most spoons of the Middle Ages had fairly short stems. Now the stems had to be made longer so that people could get food safely past the ruffs and into their mouths. At the same time large soup spoons came into wider use, because people wearing ruffs couldn't risk lifting their bowls and drinking the soup.

The way people used their eating utensils was affected by other changes that took place in the 1500s. Western Europe was moving away from the narrow outlook of the Middle Ages and toward the period of creativity, exploration, and discovery known as the Renaissance.

Cities grew in size and importance and were populated by a new middle class of craftsmen and merchants. These people

Portrait of a Dutch woman wearing a ruff by Jan Antonisz van Ravesteyn (1570–1657).

Courtesy of The Metropolitan Museum of Art, Gift of Henry Goldman, 1912

began to feel ashamed of things they had done openly before. Urination and defecation came to be regarded as private activities. Both men and women started to carry handkerchiefs for blowing the nose. Plates of wood, pewter, or silver replaced the earlier trenchers of bread. And people at meals stopped drinking from a single goblet that they passed from one to another.

Confronted by these changes, Europeans felt a need for new guides to proper behavior at the table and elsewhere. Many authors responded to this need, including the Dutch thinker Erasmus. In 1530 he published a book on manners titled *On Civility in Children.* It had been written for a ten-year-old French prince, who later became King Henry II.

Erasmus' book enjoyed an immediate success. It was reprinted more than thirty times in the next six years and appeared in numerous translations throughout Europe. An English translation was issued in 1532 and quickly became a standard textbook for well-to-do young Englishmen.

Early in the book Erasmus summed up his message. "Be lenient toward the offenses of others," he advised his readers. "A companion ought not to be less dear to you because he has worse manners. There are people who make up for the awkwardness of their behavior by other gifts."

He continued: "If one of your comrades unknowingly gives offense, tell him so alone and say it kindly. That is civility."

Erasmus went on to list specific rules for proper conduct

while eating. These may seem obvious to us today, but many were new to Erasmus' readers. Here are a few examples:

Take care to cut and clean your fingernails before dining. Otherwise dirt from under the nails may get in the food.

Don't be the first to reach into the pot; only wolves and gluttons do that. And don't put your whole hand into it—use only three fingers at most.

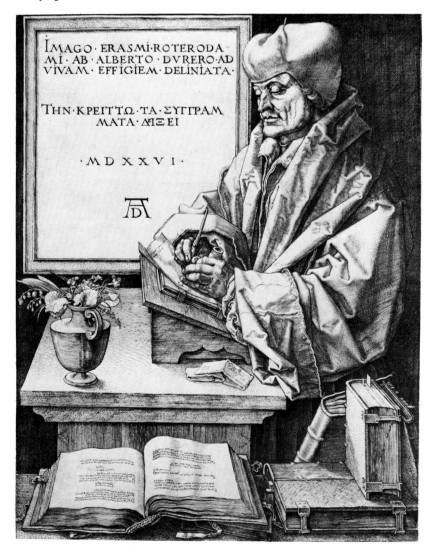

Erasmus of Rotterdam. Etching by Albrecht Dürer (1471–1528).

Courtesy of The Metropolitan Museum of Art, Fletcher Fund, 1919

Take the first piece of meat or fish that you touch, and don't poke around in the pot for a bigger one.

Don't pick your nose while eating and then reach for more food.

Don't throw bones you have chewed back in the pot. Put them on the table or toss them on the floor.

Don't clean your teeth with your knife.

If your fingers become greasy, it is not polite to lick them or wipe them on your coat. Bring a cloth along for this purpose if your host does not provide one. Or else wipe them on the tablecloth.

As more and more people adopted Erasmus' rules, table manners in Europe became more refined. But they still seemed crude to those who lived on the other side of the world, in China and Japan. "What barbarians!" a Chinese writer said when he saw some visiting Europeans using knives. "They eat with swords!"

Over the centuries, the Chinese and Japanese had developed a very different way of cooking and eating. It was based almost entirely on the use of two long, thin pieces of wood called chopsticks.

CHAPTER FOUR

The Quick Little Fellows

NO ONE KNOWS EXACTLY when the Chinese began to use chopsticks. But some say it was greedy people who thought of them first.

According to this story, it happened at the beginning of Chinese written history, around 3000 B.C., when most people cooked their food in tripods. These were metal pots that stood on three squat legs and could be set directly over a fire.

The large pots took an hour or so to cool after the food was cooked, and some people were too greedy to wait. Grabbing a pair of sticks, they poked at the steaming food and lifted out the best pieces for themselves. Others copied them, and within a short time people all over China were eating with chopsticks.

Another explanation credits the Chinese preference for chopsticks over knives to the philosopher Confucius, who lived from 551 to 479 B.C. Confucius once remarked that honorable and upright people would rather see an animal alive than dead. And if they heard the noise and screams of an animal being killed, they would not want to eat its flesh.

For Confucius, knives were a constant reminder of such killings. Consequently, he wrote in one of his books: "The honorable and upright man keeps well away from both the slaughterhouse and the kitchen, and he allows no knives on his table."

Whether or not Confucius was responsible, we do know that by 400 B.C. people throughout China were using chopsticks. Hand in hand with their adoption came the development of a uniquely Chinese style of cooking. Meat and vegetables were either cut into bite-sized pieces or cooked until they were so tender that they required no cutting. Even when poultry and fish were served whole, the meat was so tender that it could be picked easily off the bones with a pair of chopsticks.

Besides chopsticks, the Chinese from very early in their history also used spoons. They were made of a hard earthenware called porcelain, and they had flat bottoms so that a diner could set one down on a table top without spilling the contents. The Chinese thought the round-bottomed European spoon was very inefficient!

Unlike Europeans, the Chinese never used their spoons to eat any food except soup. For everything else they used chopsticks, manipulating the two sticks smoothly and quickly as they plucked bits of food from first one dish and then another. In fact, the word for chopsticks in Chinese means "the quick little fellows."

Most Chinese chopsticks are ten to twelve inches long and about as thick as a pencil. Those for children can be as short as five inches. Those used by the hostess or host to pass special delicacies to their guests are sometimes as long as twenty inches.

Chopsticks have been made from many different materials over the centuries: bamboo, wood, jade, ivory, gold, and silver. Many upper-class families in old China used ivory chopsticks tipped with silver. Since ancient times the Chinese had believed that silver was a protection against poison. If the silver-tipped chopsticks came into contact with food that had been poisoned, they would turn black—or so people said.

Only the wealthiest Chinese families could afford gold or silver chopsticks, and one had to have strong fingers to use them, for they were extremely heavy. In the classic Chinese novel *The Dream of the Red Chamber*, that fact became embarrassingly clear to a peasant girl who was dining in a wealthy home for the first time. When she tried to pick up a pigeon's egg with her gold chopsticks, she was so startled by their weight that she dropped the egg on the floor.

In setting a Chinese table, the chopsticks are placed either to the right or below a small, central plate. The soup bowl is

Chinese workers eating rice with chopsticks at Kunming airbase, 1944.

Courtesy of The
New York Public Library
Picture Collection

located to the upper right of the plate with the flat-bottomed soup spoon in it. A bowl of rice, served with every Chinese meal, is put directly on the plate.

At Chinese banquets, the meat and vegetable dishes are served one after another, and the guests help themselves to portions of each, putting them on their small plates. The soup is served last. At family dinners, all the dishes are in the middle of the table at the beginning of the meal, with the soup tureen in the center.

A single pair of chopsticks is used to eat all the dishes, even at banquets. Often the diners are provided with small rests of porcelain on which they can lay their chopsticks between courses so that they won't soil the tablecloth.

Chopsticks serve as signals during a Chinese meal. At the start, the host raises his chopsticks over his rice bowl to invite the guests to begin eating. Then he puts his rice bowl to one side of the plate, and all the other diners do the same. At the end of the meal, the diners set their chopsticks even and parallel across the tops of their rice bowls to indicate that they've finished.

Chopsticks often seem awkward to handle at first, even for Chinese children. But when you learn how to hold them firmly but lightly, there's no strain at all, and their use quickly becomes second nature.

To begin, hold your right hand (or your left, if you're left-handed) in a relaxed position. Place the first chopstick between the tip of your fourth, or ring, finger and the base of your thumb. Be sure you pick up the chopstick the right way: The top half, which you hold in your hand, is squared; the tip, which takes up the food, is rounded. Your thumb should be around the squared section and your ring finger at the midpoint of the chopstick.

Brace the chopstick against the fourth finger with the middle of the thumb, but keep the tip of the thumb free. You'll need it to help hold the second chopstick. Place the second stick between your thumbtip and the tips of your index and middle fingers. Grasp the stick lightly so that you can move it up and down against the other chopstick, which remains still.

When you want to pick up a piece of food, push upward on the second chopstick with your middle finger. This will open the tips of the chopsticks. To grasp the food, push down on the second stick with the same middle finger. The two chopsticks will come together with the food pinched securely between the two tips. Then you can raise the bite swiftly to your mouth.

It's important to keep the tips of the chopsticks even with one another at all times. If one is higher and one is lower, the chopsticks will not work.

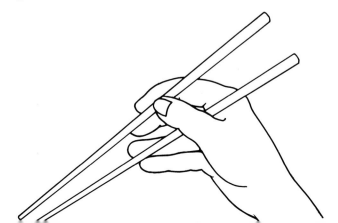

Illustration by Pat Tobin

Rice is hard to eat with chopsticks because the individual grains are so small. However, the Chinese have found a solution to this problem. They lift the rice bowl with their thumb resting on the rim and their index and middle fingers grasping the bottom. Then, holding the bowl quite close to the mouth, they use their chopsticks to transfer globs of rice from bowl to mouth. When they get near the bottom of the bowl, they raise it up to the lips in a drinking position and scoop out the last few grains.

The use of chopsticks spread from China to the neighboring countries of Vietnam and Korea. Eventually, like many other Chinese customs, it also reached Japan. This occurred sometime before A.D. 500, and within a short time people throughout the Japanese islands were eating with chopsticks.

The Japanese called their chopsticks *hashi*, meaning bridge, because the sticks acted as a bridge between bowl and mouth. Japanese chopsticks differed somewhat from the Chinese variety. They had tapered rather than rounded ends, and were most often made of lacquered wood instead of bamboo or ivory.

Lacquer is obtained from the juice of a tree peculiar to the Far East, and is purified by filtering. The lacquer, which may be colored, is then applied to chopsticks or other wooden objects in several successive layers. After the lacquer dries, the chopsticks are rubbed down to give them a smooth, shiny surface. If the layers of lacquer are thick enough, they can be carved, painted, or engraved. Many lacquered Japanese chopsticks feature beautiful inlaid designs of gilt or mother-of-pearl.

Besides their use at table, chopsticks also play a role in the cremation ceremonies of Japanese Buddhists. This has led to certain dining taboos. For example, a Japanese never passes food to another person with his own chopsticks. This might remind the person of the Buddhist ritual in which bone fragments of the deceased are picked from the funeral pyre with ceremonial chopsticks and passed among the family members.

The Japanese never stick their chopsticks upright in a bowl of rice either, since that action also has a connection with death. Buddhist mourners customarily place a bowl of uncooked rice by the family altar as an offering to the deceased, and then stand his chopsticks upright in it.

The Japanese observe other taboos when using chopsticks. If they go on a picnic, they take along disposable wooden chopsticks, and always break them in two when they've finished eating. Otherwise, they believe, a wily devil might find the chopsticks and use them for some evil purpose.

Basically, though, the Japanese handle their chopsticks in the same way the Chinese do. And they've done so for centuries. When a merchant from Italy, Francesco Carletti, visited Japan at the end of the 1500s, he wrote in his journal about the natives' skillful use of chopsticks.

19th-century Japanese family at dinner.

Courtesy of The Kubler Picture Collection, Cooper-Hewitt Museum, Smithsonian Institution/Art Resource

"They are the length of a man's hand and as thick as a quill for writing," wrote Carletti. "With these two sticks, the Japanese are able to fill their mouths with marvelous swiftness and agility. They can pick up any piece of food, no matter how tiny it is, without ever soiling their hands."

Carletti was writing at a time when most Europeans still ate with their fingers. But that would soon change. A new utensil was about to be introduced on dinner tables from Italy to England. This utensil would enable Europeans to eat their food as neatly and cleanly as the Japanese diners Carletti had observed. Eventually it would revolutionize Western table manners.

What was this wonder-working utensil? The common fork.

CHAPTER FIVE

The Fork Comes
to the Table

ABOUT THE YEAR 1000, according to an Italian story, a wealthy nobleman from Venice, the great trading city, met a beautiful Turkish princess while he was traveling in the Middle East. After a brief courtship, the nobleman married the princess and returned with her to Venice.

Along with her jewels, the princess' luggage contained a case of table forks. Forks had been in common use in the royal courts of the Middle East since at least the seventh century, and the princess had eaten with them all her life.

The first fork was probably a crotched stick with the two prongs sharpened at the end. Early people must have discovered that natural forks like this came in handy when they were roasting meat over a fire. The first metal forks were massive

*Two-pronged
Roman fork made of
bronze.*

Courtesy of The
Metropolitan Museum
of Art, Bequest of
Richard B. Seager, 1926

ones made of bronze that the ancient Egyptians used to lift sacrificial offerings of food in religious ceremonies.

The Greeks and Romans also had ceremonial forks, and large, two-pronged kitchen forks. Some small silver forks have even been found in the ruins of Pompeii and Herculaneum, two Roman cities that were buried by the volcanic eruption of Mount Vesuvius in A.D. 79. But there is no record of people eating with forks until they began to appear on wealthy tables in the Middle East in the 600s.

The princess' forks created a sensation when she set them out in the dining room of her new home in Venice. One observer commented: "Instead of eating with her fingers like other people, the princess cuts up her food into small pieces and eats them by means of little golden forks with two prongs." Another called her behavior "luxurious beyond belief."

The church leaders of Venice were even more shocked. "God in his wisdom has provided man with natural forks—his fingers," said one. "Therefore it is an insult to Him to substitute artificial metallic forks for them when eating."

Shortly afterward, according to the story, the princess was afflicted with a terrible illness and died. Some declared solemnly that it was God's will. Others said it was because she insisted on eating with a fork. Whatever the explanation, it would be another three hundred years before the use of the fork at table became common in Italy. Meanwhile, European cooks continued to carve and serve meat with the help of large, two-pronged forks, as they had since the days of the Roman Empire.

In 1361, table forks were listed for the first time in an inventory of silverware owned by the council of the Italian city of Florence. Italian cookbooks began to mention table forks in the late 1400s. And in 1533 Catherine de Médici, daughter of the ruler of Florence, introduced the fork to France. The fourteen-year-old Catherine brought several dozen with her to Paris when she married the future French King Henry II.

Many Frenchmen thought it was affected to eat with a fork. They laughed when they heard that some diners at Henry II's court, who were unfamiliar with the utensil, allowed half the food to fall off their fork between plate and mouth. But gradually the use of table forks spread out from the King's palace to wealthy homes throughout France.

It took longer for the fork to reach England, perhaps because the island British were traditionally suspicious of things that came from abroad. Thomas Coryate, who had traveled widely in Italy and France, claimed in a book published in 1611 that he was the first man in London to eat with a fork.

His friends made fun of him, Coryate wrote, and called him *furciferus*, which meant "pitchfork handler." To which Coryate replied, "Wait and see; one day you each will have a fork. Mark my words!"

And he was right. Within a few years, every member of the British royal family and the court possessed a fork. By the

Utensils with detachable handles and leather carrying cases. France and Italy, 16th and 17th centuries.

Courtesy of The Cooper-Hewitt Museum, Smithsonian Institution—The Robert L. Metzenberg Collection, Gift of Eleanor L. Metzenberg

mid-1600s, eating with a fork had become the fashion among British taste makers and the nobility. From them the practice trickled down to the merchants and craftsmen, and eventually to the poor—as styles and customs usually did.

Cutlery centers such as Sheffield, England, now produced large numbers of forks along with knives and spoons. Like spoons, forks could either be cast in molds or stamped from bars of metal. Their prongs, called tines, were usually made of steel or silver, while the handles might be carved from precious or semiprecious materials like rock crystal and ivory. Among the rich, the beauty and rarity of one's personal eating utensils had long been a mark of social status.

When European nobles and wealthier commoners went on trips, they often carried their cutlery with them, just as we carry our toothbrushes. This was not due to fastidiousness, but simply because many inns of the time still did not provide guests with utensils. Travelers wanted their luggage to be as compact as possible, so the makers of cutlery developed knives, forks, and spoons that could be folded, or that had interlocking handles. These fitted into small, specially designed cases of leather or metal.

At first most table forks had only two long, flat tines. But by the end of the 1600s, English and Continental cutlers had started to manufacture forks with three and four tines, and to give them a slight curve. The additional tines enabled diners to pick up meat and vegetables more easily, and the curve made the fork a more efficient scoop.

The widespread adoption of the table fork affected the design of both spoons and knives. Before the 1600s, most European spoons were of a single size. They had large, fig-shaped bowls and rounded stems, and were used to bring to the mouth everything from soup to stew. Now spoons began to take on the egg-shaped bowls and flat stems that we're familiar with today.

The new-style spoons came in two basic sizes. The larger ones were called tablespoons, and the smaller ones teaspoons. Tea had arrived in Europe for the first time early in the seventeenth century as trade with the Far East expanded. Coffee reached Europe at about the same time, brought by Italian merchant seamen who traded with Turkey. People felt the need of a smaller spoon to stir the popular new beverages, so they invented the teaspoon.

The design of table knives changed even more noticeably. Now that people throughout Europe were eating with forks, they no longer needed knives with sharp points to spear their food. Consequently, by the end of the seventeenth century most European table knives were made with rounded ends.

Knife and fork with matching ivory handles. German, 17th century.

Courtesy of Bayerisches National-museum, Munich

A

A royal feast at the French court in the time of Cardinal Richelieu. Engraving by Abraham Bosse, 1633.

Some say Cardinal Richelieu, a French religious and political leader, was responsible for this change in knife design. The Cardinal frequently entertained at dinner a nobleman who was in the habit of picking his teeth with the point of his knife. Disgusted with the man's behavior, the Cardinal had the points of all his table knives ground down, and others in the French court followed the Cardinal's lead.

Whether that story is true or not, it's known that in 1669 King Louis XIV of France, in order to discourage violence, made it illegal for anyone to carry a pointed knife, for cutlers to make them, or for innkeepers to put them on their tables. The King further commanded that the points of all existing table knives be rounded off. Frenchmen were quick to obey, and the new style in knife design traveled rapidly to England, Holland, Belgium, and other European countries.

Besides influencing knife design, Louis XIV became the first host in Europe to provide his guests with a complete table setting. No longer did visitors to one of Louis's palaces have to bring their own utensils with them. Instead, when they sat down to dinner, they could use the handsome silver knives, forks, and spoons, all bearing the royal insignia, that were laid at every place. Louis himself always ate with utensils made of gold; it was one of the reasons he was called "the Sun King."

From France, the custom of providing table utensils spread to the other royal courts of Europe, and from them to the houses of the nobility. As the seventeenth century drew to an end, well-to-do people everywhere were buying matching sets of flatware—knives, forks, and spoons—for their tables. Most of these sets were made of silver.

In less than a hundred years, the way people ate in Europe had changed more than it had in the previous thousand. Not only had the fork been introduced, and the shape of knives and spoons been drastically altered, but plates had replaced trenchers, and many families now owned flatware. For the first time since the days of the Roman Empire, diners in wealthy homes were given napkins as a matter of course.

To reflect all these changes, new books on table manners

An upper-class French family at breakfast. Engraving by Lepicié, after a painting by François Boucher (1703–1770).

Courtesy of The Metropolitan Museum of Art, The Elisha Whittelsey Fund, 1950

were needed, and they soon began to appear. In 1729 a French priest published a guide to behavior for young gentlemen. In it he wrote: "At table you should always use a napkin, a plate, a knife, a spoon, and a fork. It is improper to use the napkin to wipe your face or rub your teeth clean, and it would be one of the grossest offenses against civility to use it to blow your nose. The only use you may make of the napkin is to wipe your mouth, lips, and fingers when they become soiled."

The priest continued: "It is polite always to use the fork to put meat into your mouth for propriety does not permit the touching of anything greasy with the fingers." How different from the advice Erasmus had given his young readers just two hundred years earlier! Then you were expected to eat meat with your fingers. Now such behavior was thought to be offensive and uncivilized.

Another Frenchman, writing in 1765, summed up the changes that had occurred. "If people who died in 1700 could come back to life," he wrote, "they would not recognize Paris as far as its table manners are concerned."

More changes were soon to come. The Industrial Revolution, which started in England in the late 1700s, would spur the growth of mass production, including the manufacture of table utensils. And the people of a new nation, the United States of America, would develop their own unique way of using those utensils.

⊠⊠⊠⊠

CHAPTER SIX

The Rise and Fall of Table Manners

A WELL-TO-DO BRITISH MERCHANT and his family are having supper in the dining room of their London town house on a fine
spring evening in 1700. The soup course has been finished,
and now the maid brings in the main course: a steaming roast
of beef accompanied by boiled potatoes and peas.

The merchant carves thick slices of meat for his wife, son,
daughter, and himself, and everyone begins to eat. Since they're
all right-handed, they take their forks in their left hands and
jab them into the meat with the tines curved downward. They
pick up their knives with their right hands and cut off pieces
of meat. Then, with their forks still held in their left hands,
they quickly bring the meat to their mouths.

This method of handling the knife and fork is called the
Continental style. It has been employed in England and on

the European continent ever since forks came into common use and knives were rounded. But while the London merchant of 1700 was using the Continental style to eat his roast beef, his counterpart in Boston, far across the ocean in the British colony of Massachusetts, was employing a very different method.

The Boston merchant, dining with his family in their home on Beacon Hill, does not yet have any forks. When he came as a boy to Massachusetts with his parents in 1660, the family was still eating with spoons and sharp-pointed knives only. They used the spoon to hold down their slices of beef or lamb while they cut off a piece of meat with the knife. Then they raised the meat to their mouths on the sharp point of the knife.

Now, although the merchant has heard of forks, he hasn't ordered any from England. However, the knives he imports are of the new, rounded type and can no longer be used to spear pieces of meat. So the merchant—along with most other people in the American colonies—has worked out a new way of eating. He still uses a spoon to steady the meat as he cuts it with a rounded knife. But then he sets down the knife, switches the spoon to his right hand, and uses the spoon to lift the meat to his mouth.

When wealthy people in the colonies finally did begin to import table forks from England in the mid-1700s, they used them in the same way they were accustomed to using spoons. They held down the meat with a fork just as the English and

Europeans did, but instead of raising the pieces immediately to their mouths, they transferred the fork to their right hand first. This became known as the American style of eating, and most people in the United States still follow it today.

By 1800, almost every American family was using forks, but a few still considered them an affectation. "Eating peas with a fork," said one man in Maine, "is as bad as trying to eat soup with a knitting needle." He insisted on eating his peas with one of the old-fashioned pointed knives and claimed it was far more efficient.

Meanwhile, in the royal courts of Europe and the homes of the nobility, more and more utensils were being developed, each with its own special purpose. There were short forks for eating salad and longer forks for eating meat; small, blunt butter knives and oddly shaped fish knives. There were large-bowled spoons for eating soup, and long-handled spoons with small bowls for eating desserts such as parfaits that were served in tall glass dishes.

Dining in the homes of the rich became an ever more elaborate ritual in the early 1800s. But people living on small European farms or in city slums were lucky if they had a few bent, scarred utensils to eat their potatoes, bread, and soup. When they could afford a bit of meat, many still ate it with their fingers and wiped their greasy hands on their sleeves.

Thanksgiving dinner in a New England farmhouse, mid-1800s. From a drawing by F. A. Chapman.

Courtesy of The Kubler Picture Collection, Cooper-Hewitt Museum, Smithsonian Institution/Art Resource

The Industrial Revolution soon changed all that. As factories sprang up in Europe and America and new techniques of mass production were developed, many items that had once been luxuries came within reach of almost everyone. Among these were matching sets of table utensils.

In the new factories, processes formerly done by hand were now done by steam-powered machines. High-quality knife blades were forged from bars of steel by mechanical hammers. Other machines made spoons and forks by cutting large sheets of metal into strips of the required width and length. The strips—called blanks—were then fed into presses that gave each spoon or fork its rough shape, one end being almost square for a spoon and rectangular for a fork.

Women immigrants eating with their fingers on Ward's Island, New York, 1870.

Courtesy of The Kubler Picture Collection, Cooper-Hewitt Museum, Smithsonian Institution/Art Resource

After being trimmed, the spoon blanks were placed between steel dies. The dies, driven together with great force, hollowed out the bowls of the spoons and stamped patterns on their handles.

In the case of forks, machines first cut out slots in the blanks to form the tines. Then steel dies stamped the forks to the proper curvature, and abrasive belts pointed and sharpened the tines.

Although some expensive sets of silver tableware, and a few of gold, were still being manufactured, most of the new mass-produced utensils were silver plated. This was done by a process called electroplating, which was invented in the 1840s.

In the electroplating process, a thin coating of silver was applied to an inexpensive base metal such as copper or nickel by means of an electric current. After 1860, historians estimate, 90 percent of the silverware manufactured in Britain and America was electroplated.

As silverware became more affordable, special types were made just for fun. Souvenir spoons, for example, were extremely popular in America starting in the mid-1800s. When people visited a famous site like Niagara Falls or a European capital like London or Paris, they could buy a souvenir spoon with some of the main features of the place engraved on its bowl and stem.

While souvenir spoons made nice decorations, people were more interested in sets of beautiful silverware that would last

Silver souvenir spoon from Austria, 19th century.

Courtesy of The Metropolitan Museum of Art, Gift of Sir W. H. Redding, 1908

all their lives and could be handed down to their children. In the early years of the twentieth century, scientists perfected a durable new material for flatware—stainless steel. An alloy of steel and chromium, stainless steel successfully resisted the corrosion and rust caused by common household acids and alkalis. Designers responded to the new material by creating stainless steel tableware in a variety of clean-lined modern styles.

Many people continued to want silver-plated flatware, however, and they preferred more traditional designs. A bride-to-be selected a pattern at a specialty or department store and registered it with the sales clerks. Then the bride's friends and relatives would know what pieces she needed when they came in to buy wedding gifts. It was customary to give a complete place setting: a tablespoon and teaspoon; a dinner knife and butter knife; a dinner fork and a salad fork.

The placement of the utensils on the table became standard in America, and indicated the order in which they were to be used. Forks were always put to the left of the plate, and there were often two: a longer dinner fork and a shorter salad fork. If the salad fork was placed to the left of the larger fork, it meant that it was to be used for the salad, which might already be on the table. However, if it was placed to the right of the larger fork, then it meant that the salad would be served later, as part of the main course or afterward, or that the smaller fork was to be used for dessert.

The butter knife would be found on the bread and butter plate, which was usually set on the table just above the forks. This knife was positioned either across the bread and butter plate or along its right side.

The long dinner knife was always placed to the right of the dinner plate, its blade turned inward toward the plate. If steak or another thick cut of meat was to be served, there might also be a steak knife with an especially sharp, notched edge. It was to be used for cutting the meat and nothing else.

Spoons appeared to the right of the dinner knife in order of expected use, like the forks. For instance, if a large spoon was placed to the right of a teaspoon, that meant the first course would be soup. If a large spoon was placed between the knife and a teaspoon, it was probably intended for dessert—although it might be for soup if a fruit cup or other appetizer requiring a teaspoon was served first. The diner would just have to wait and see.

As the middle class grew in the late nineteenth and early twentieth centuries, and more and more families purchased sets of tableware, there arose a fresh demand for guides to

A standard place setting.

Illustration by Pat Tobin

etiquette and table manners. Some were written especially for children, including *The Goops* by Gelett Burgess. Published in 1900, Burgess' book proved to be immensely popular and was reprinted many times. In the section on table manners, Burgess described his imaginary creatures as follows:

> *The Goops they lick their fingers,*
> *And the Goops they lick their knives;*
> *They spill their broth on the tablecloth—*
> *Oh, they lead disgusting lives!*
> *The Goops they talk while eating,*
> *And loud and fast they chew;*
> *And that is why I'm glad that I*
> *Am not a Goop—are you?*

One of the most successful guides for adults was *Etiquette* by Emily Post, published in the first of many editions in 1922. Many of its precepts are still being observed today. Mrs. Post wrote: "All rules of table manners are made to avoid ugliness; to let anyone see what you have in your mouth is repulsive; to make a noise is to suggest an animal; to make a mess is disgusting."

With regard to table utensils, Mrs. Post and others said that once a piece of silver had been used, it should never again be put back on the table because it might soil the tablecloth. Soup is usually served with a plate under the bowl. If so, the soup spoon should be put on the plate; if not, the spoon can be put in the bowl after the diner finishes eating. The butter knife is to remain on the bread and butter plate at all times, and the salad fork should stay on the salad plate when not in use.

Diners were warned never to leave the dinner knife and fork hanging over the rim of the plate with the handles on the table. Instead, when the knife is not being used to cut food it should be placed across the upper edge of the plate, diagonal to the edge of the table and with the blade turned toward the center of the plate. The fork, when not in use, should also be laid diagonally across the upper edge of the plate, next to the knife and with the tines turned upward.

When a diner finished a course, he was told to place both knife and fork across the center of the plate, parallel to the edge of the table. This would signal that he was through eating and the plate could be removed.

Mrs. Post and other writers on table manners also gave instructions on how to handle the utensils. Normally the fork handle is held between thumb and forefinger, with the other three fingers in a relaxed position helping to support the fork. For most eating activities, the tines are turned upward.

The knife is held sideways, with the sharp edge of the blade pointed downward. The thumb and last three fingers are curved around the handle of the knife, while the index finger is held firmly along the upper edge to apply pressure in cutting.

Diners in the 1950s eating soup in the correct way.

Courtesy of The Bettmann Archive, Inc.

Mrs. Post remarked that small children often clutch their spoons in their fists. They should be taught that the proper way to hold a spoon is with the end of the stem resting on the side of the curved index finger, supported by the other three fingers. The thumb presses down on the top of the stem and helps to keep the spoon steady.

Spoons are always held horizontally, the bowls turned upward, except when they are being used for stirring. When a diner is eating soup, he should dip the spoon away from him. The spoon should also be filled no more than two thirds full, to lessen the chance of spilling the liquid on the way from bowl to mouth.

Regardless of the food, Mrs. Post and the other writers advised diners never to take up more than one mouthful on their spoons. Sipping or nibbling a little at a time from the spoon was said to be both improper and unattractive.

The writers also mentioned many specific foods and the utensils that should be used to eat them. When in doubt, the fork is always the utensil of choice. It can be used alone to eat most fish, casseroles, meats, and vegetables, and many desserts. A fork should also be used by itself to pick up spaghetti from the plate by twirling the strands around the tines, and not by bracing the fork against a soupspoon as was once recommended.

Except for watermelon, melons are usually eaten with a

spoon. Watermelon is generally eaten with a fork. The butter knife is to be used only to spread butter on bread, rolls, or crackers. It should never be used to put butter on potatoes or vegetables, with one exception—corn on the cob.

Diners were told never to pick up a piece of chicken or a chop to finish the meat on it unless they were at a picnic or a barbecue, or unless the hostess or host did so first. If they didn't, diners were advised to remove as much meat as they could with their knives and forks and leave the rest.

Eating with the fingers might be tempting, but diners were warned that it was unacceptable at the table except for what are known as "finger foods." These include some fruits, such as grapes; sandwiches, unless they are served open faced; potato chips; small cakes, cookies, nuts, and candies. Deviled eggs are considered to be finger food. So is pizza, although it can also be eaten with a knife and fork if it is hot or has a very thick crust.

At a formal dinner, however, almost nothing qualifies as a finger food.

In recent years, people in America and elsewhere have grown impatient with such formality at mealtimes. Few families have servants today, the pace of life has quickened, and many feel there are more important things to worry about than which fork to use. In homes and restaurants, diners are often expected to retain one basic set of utensils and use it for all the courses. With the spread of fast-food restaurants, even one set of utensils may not be necessary.

Now, for the first time since the 1600s, millions of people in the Western world are ignoring table manners and eating with their fingers again.

⊠⊠⊠⊠

CHAPTER SEVEN

Forks in Tokyo, Chopsticks in Chicago

IT IS 7:30 A.M. on a schoolday, and eleven-year-old David is running late. His parents have already left for the long commute to their jobs in the city, and David's school bus will be coming down the road in less than ten minutes.

David knows he should eat a bowl of cereal—in fact, Mom left him a reminder on the refrigerator—but there just isn't time. Instead he pours out a small glass of orange juice and a large glass of milk, and swigs them down between bites of a banana he found on the counter. Then, grabbing his backpack and a doughnut, he hurries out of the house and down the road to the bus stop. In eating his breakfast, David didn't use a single utensil.

The main course at lunch in the school cafeteria is a hot dog, served with baked beans on a paper plate. From habit,

David picks up a set of plastic utensils—knife, fork, and spoon—on his way to the table, and as things turn out he needs them all to eat his beans. First the handle of the fork breaks off, and then the handle of the spoon. Forgetting his table manners, David scoops up the remaining beans on his knife, like a boy in the Middle Ages.

That evening Dad has to stay on in the city for a business dinner, and Mom is late getting home. She and David decide to have a light, quick supper in the recreation room while they watch TV. David helps her make ham and cheese sandwiches and pours out two glasses of milk. For dessert they eat a couple of crisp, red apples. The kitchen drawers are filled with stainless steel utensils, but neither David nor his mother uses any of them.

Like David and his mother, many people eat on the run today. Everyone operates on his or her own schedule. They often fail to get together even for the traditional evening meal, at which families once gathered to share their experiences of the day while they observed good manners.

Table manners have also suffered from the rebellious mood of the 1960s and 1970s. In those years, people questioned the need for rules and structure in many different areas of life. They believed that it was better to be natural than to be civilized, and made fun of people who still thought it was important to know when and how to use their knives and forks.

As a result, many people today, both young and old, feel embarrassed and confused when they find themselves in an unfamiliar dining situation. For example, a fifteen-year-old boy from a Chicago suburb confessed that before he left home for boarding school he ate "like a slob."

"Once I went to a big dinner meeting with my father," the boy said, "and when they served spaghetti I didn't know what to do, so I ate it with my hands. I just slurped it up and put it in my mouth. Believe me, my dad took some grief about that."

People in other parts of the world are having trouble with their table utensils too. As American-style fast-food restaurants become more popular in Japan, parents there fear that their children won't learn how to use chopsticks correctly.

Research conducted in 1935 showed that most Japanese youngsters mastered the use of chopsticks by the age of three. Now the average age is six, and many never attain the skill at all. To conceal their lack of technique, and avoid accidents, these children often keep their heads close to the plate. This is called eating "dog-style." Some children even spear their food with chopsticks, which is as unacceptable in Japan as eating peas with a knife is in the United States.

Many Japanese blame the chopstick decline on the spread of Western foods in Japan and the need to eat them with a knife and fork. In fact, Japanese children today often learn to eat with a special implement that has a spoon on one end and a fork on the other.

Other Japanese commentators say the fault lies with the nation's educational system. They claim that it places so much emphasis on test taking that there's little time left to teach Japanese children the basic skills required for daily living.

Still others maintain that neither Western food nor poor schooling is to blame. "It's parents who are the cause of the problem," says a Japanese professor of preschool education. "They themselves never learned how to handle chopsticks properly, so how can they teach their children?"

Many Japanese organizations and businesses are taking steps to improve the situation. The Tokyo police department gives new recruits a crash course in chopstick use and etiquette.

A Japanese boy uses chopsticks incorrectly by crossing them instead of holding them even.

Courtesy of Haruyoshi Yamaguchi, New York Times Pictures

Corporations offer their employees two hours of chopstick training every week for three months. And Japanese supermarkets and department stores now stock "trainer chopsticks," plastic devices with loops to show children where to put their fingers. In 1984, one manufacturer of trainer chopsticks reported sales of 10,000 pairs a day.

People in the United States and other parts of the Western world are trying to halt the decline of table manners in their countries, too. Practical, up-to-date books like *Miss Manners' Guide to Excruciatingly Correct Behavior* by Judith Martin have become best sellers. Recently a national network of etiquette consultants has sprung up in the U.S. These consultants lecture regularly at the major business schools and fly all over the country to conduct special courses in table behavior for young executives.

"Table manners are crucial," said one executive who took such a course. "When you have an important client and the possibility for a big sale, you don't want to blow the opportunity by spilling your soup or putting your dirty knife down on the tablecloth."

In recent years, there's also been a trend toward the transfer of eating utensils from one culture to another. Just as many Japanese now eat some foods with forks, so more and more Americans are attempting to use chopsticks when they go out to a Chinese, Japanese, Vietnamese, or Korean restaurant, or when they cook Oriental foods at home. They say that sweet-and-sour pork and sushi taste much better when eaten with chopsticks.

On the other hand, the Chinese, who invented chopsticks, are questioning whether they're always the best utensil for eating. Through the centuries Chinese families have traditionally dipped their personal chopsticks straight into a single serving pot. Now some Chinese doctors are saying that this practice helps to spread infectious diseases such as hepatitis.

The former Chairman of the Chinese Communist Party,

A Chinese man tries eating with a fork.

Courtesy of UPI/
Bettmann Newsphotos

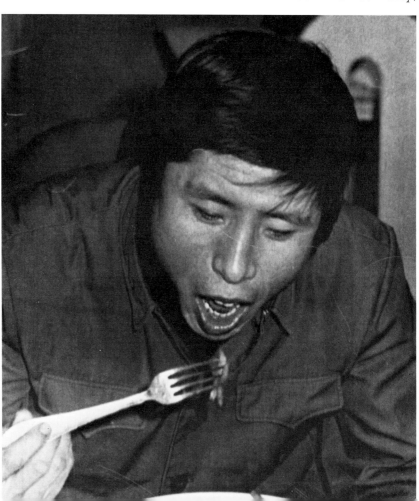

Hu Yaobang, joined in the discussion. "We should prepare more knives and forks, buy more plates, and sit around the table to eat Chinese food in the Western manner, that is, each from his own plate," Chairman Hu said in a 1984 speech. "By doing so we can avoid many contagious diseases."

It's doubtful, however, whether the Chinese people will soon give up a style of eating that has endured for at least 2500 years. It's equally doubtful that a majority of Westerners will ever put aside their knives and forks in favor of chopsticks.

What's more likely is that people everywhere will continue to experiment with one another's table utensils. And who knows? Perhaps in time they will find a common solution to that age-old problem: how to get food as swiftly, gracefully, and neatly as possible from hand to mouth.

Bibliography

*Those titles marked with * were written for children.*

Arnott, Margaret L., editor. *Gastronomy: The Anthropology of Food and Food Habits.* The Hague and Paris: Mouton Publishers, 1975.

Bailey, C. T. P. *Knives and Forks.* London and Boston: The Medici Society, 1927.

Bement, Lewis D. *The Cutlery Story.* Dalton, Georgia: Custom Cutlery, Inc., 1950.

*Berry, Erick. *Eating and Cooking Around the World: Fingers Before Forks.* New York: The John Day Company, 1963.

Boger, Ann C. *Consuming Passions: The Art of Food and Drink.* Cleveland: The Cleveland Museum of Art, 1983.

Braudel, Fernand. *The Structures of Everyday Life: The Limits of the Possible.* New York: Harper & Row, 1981.

Brennan, Jennifer. *The Cuisines of Asia.* New York: St. Martin's/Marek, 1984.

Brett, Gerard. *Dinner Is Served.* Hamden, Connecticut: Archon Books, 1969.

Burns, John F. "New Chinese Imperative Attacks Chopsticks." Article in *The New York Times*, December 24, 1984.

Chang, Cecelia Sun Yun. *The Mandarin Way.* Boston: The Atlantic Monthly Press, 1974.

Chang, K. C., editor. *Food in Chinese Culture.* New Haven and London: Yale University Press, 1977.

The Editors of "China Pictorial," The People's Republic of China. *Chinese Cuisine from the Master Chefs of China.* Boston: Little, Brown and Company, 1983.

Chu, Grace Zia. *Madame Chu's Chinese Cooking School.* New York: Simon and Schuster, 1975.

Claiborne, Craig. "Chopsticks: An Insight." Article in *The New York Times,* August 6, 1979.

Deetz, James. *In Small Things Forgotten: The Archeology of Early American Life.* Garden City, New York: Anchor Books, 1977.

Discover Japan, Volume 1. Tokyo, New York, and San Francisco: Kodansha International, 1982.

Elias, Norbert. *The Civilizing Process: The History of Manners.* New York: Urizen Books, 1978.

Emery, John. *European Spoons Before 1700.* Edinburgh: John Donald Publishers, Ltd., 1976.

Farb, Peter, and George Armelagos. *Consuming Passions.* Boston: Houghton Mifflin Company, 1980.

Greer, William R. "Table Manners: A Casualty of Changing Times." Article in *The New York Times,* October 16, 1985.

Hampson, John. *The English at Table.* London: William Collins, 1944.

Houart, Victor. *Antique Spoons: A Collector's Guide.* London: Souvenir Press, 1982.

Latham, Jean. *The Pleasure of Your Company: A History of Manners and Meals.* London: Adam & Charles Black, 1972.

Lo, Kenneth. *The Encyclopedia of Chinese Cooking.* New York: A and W Publishers, 1982.

Martin, Judith. *Miss Manners' Guide to Excruciatingly Correct Behavior.* New York: Atheneum, 1982.

Miller, Gloria Bley. *The Thousand Recipe Chinese Cookbook*. New York: Grosset and Dunlap, 1970.

Needham, Joseph. *Science and Civilization in China*, Volume IV. London: Cambridge University Press, 1965.

*Perl, Lila. *Ethiopia: Land of the Lion*. New York: William Morrow and Company, 1972.

Pullar, Philippa. *Consuming Passions: Being an Historic Inquiry Into Certain English Appetites*. Boston: Little, Brown and Company, 1970.

Rainwater, Dorothy T., and Donna H. Felger. *American Spoons: Souvenir and Historical*. Camden, New Jersey: Thomas Nelson and Sons; Hanover, Pennsylvania: Everybody's Press, 1968.

Rudofsky, Bernard. *Now I Lay Me Down to Eat*. Garden City, New York: Anchor Books, 1980.

Snodin, Michael, and Gail Belden. *Spoons*. London: Pitman Publishing, 1976.

Stern, Philip Van Doren. *Prehistoric Europe: From Stone Age Man to the Early Greeks*. New York: W. W. Norton and Company, Inc., 1969.

Stewart, Marjabelle Young. *Marjabelle Stewart's Book of Modern Table Manners*. New York: St. Martin's Press, 1981.

Tannahill, Reay. *Food in History*. New York: Stein and Day, 1973.

Tsuji, Shizuo (with the assistance of Mary Sutherland). *Japanese Cooking, a Simple Art*. Tokyo, New York, and San Francisco: Kodansha International, 1980.

Weiner, Debra. "Chopsticks: Ritual, Lore and Etiquette." Article in *The New York Times*, December 26, 1984.

White, Rose V. *Table Manners and Dining Out*. Emily Post Institute, Inc., 1963.

Wolff, Edwin Daniel. *Why We Do It*. Freeport, New York: Books for Libraries Press, 1968.

Index

Numbers in *italics* indicate illustrations.